Learning the Art of

Effective Leadership

Learning the Art of Effective Leadership

Learning the Art of Effective Leadership

Copyright © 2018 by Zebulan D. Hundley

All rights reserved.

This book or any portion thereof may not be reproduced or used in any manner whatsoever without the express written permission of the publisher except for the use of brief quotations in a book review.

Printed in the United States of America

First Printing, 2018

ISBN: 978-1984266590

Send inquiries to:

info@zebulanhundley.com

Acknowledgements

All leaders have been able to stand on the shoulders of many leaders before them. I am no exception. Had it not been for the countless hours that others have spent growing and developing as leaders, I would not have had the opportunity to grow as much as I have. While there is no possible way for me to credit all of those who have had an influential role in my development as a leader, I would be unjust without giving a special thanks to a select few.

A special thank you is in order for David Fogel–my first squad leader while in the U.S. Army. Many lessons I would later learn would be because of his welcoming advice upon my arrival to our duty station. "Always learn from leaders above you… either how to do it or how not to do it." I did not understand then how important this advice would be to my development.

A special thank you is also in order for Pastor Ken Harris of New Life Christian Ministries in Hagerstown, Maryland. Under his leadership, I first began digging into how one should lead in a volunteer organization. Through much of this experience, I derived life lessons that would later come into play when pursuing – and eventually earning – my doctorate. Had it not been for his willingness to let me figure a lot of things out in his organization, I would not be where I am today.

To Pastor Jordan Poole, Lead Pastor at Hope Church in Warner Robins- This has been an exciting journey so far! Thank you for your leadership and continued

patience and support while I knocked this project out. I'm looking forward to many more years of great things with you. Let's change the world!
www.iamhope.church

To John and Mary Beth Sanders—a very special thanks is due. From the opening of your home to the discussions around the dinner table to the welcoming of me into your family, I have learned much from your experience and insight. Your generosity and willingness to give of yourselves for the betterment of those you encounter is inspirational.

To my parents, Dan and Julie Hundley, I simply cannot express into words the thanks I have for your example, for your generosity, for your patience, and for your understanding. Thank you for the freedom I had to explore what it was to become me. Thank you for the lessons learned, the opportunities given, and for the determination I saw in you to find ways to "figure it out" when everything seemed to go against you. I hope to carry on your legacy as gracefully as you're living it out today.

To Janet Ruth at Penguin Books and HUGEOrange.com, thank you for giving your professional editing eye to this vision. You are amazing to work with and your skills are second to none! I'm sure each reader will be very appreciative of your time and energy that was put into this work.

To my children, Aiden and Keira—you two are amazing examples of how to honor and love others. The extra responsibility that you've taken on as you've grown has been noticed and is very much appreciated. You are amazing examples for others to follow and your daddy could not be any prouder of you. I love you so much!

Finally, to my wife, Jenn. They say that behind every strong man is a strong woman. While true, I feel my strongest is when you are beside me. You have stuck beside me through some of the toughest moments of my life and have somehow made them a joy. You are strong—yet gentle, steadfast—yet flexible, and a force to be reckoned with. Your words of encouragement at just the right time and your willingness to balance so much so I could be on this journey has made this possible. You are an amazing wife, partner, mother, and friend. You are an amazing you. Thank you for your prayers, your faithfulness, your kid-wrangling skills, and for that oh-so-good peach pie. I love you, Jenn. Here's to the next chapter!

Zebulan Hundley
Hawkinsville, Georgia
January 2018

Learning the Art of Effective Leadership

Table of Contents

1		Introduction	12
2		The Leader in You	15
	2.1	Your Values	16
	2.2	Your Credibility	22
	2.3	Key Questions	34
3		Your Destination	35
	3.1	Chart the Course	45
	3.2	Launch a New Initiative	60
	3.3	Make the Journey	90
	3.4	Key Questions	105
4		Your Starting Point	106
	4.1	Know Your Role	107
	4.2	Getting Buy-In	126
	4.3	Momentum	131
	4.4	Starting Over	143

	4.5	Key Questions....................................148
5		U.S. Army NCO Creed..............................149

1 INTRODUCTION

In my leadership journey, I've had the privilege of working with many types of leaders. These leaders have all come from different backgrounds, have all had different personalities, and have all approached the task of leading people from a different perspective. From each, I've learned many lessons that have been valuable and have affected my approach to leadership today. Having led in many environments, cultures, and industries, I've found a few leadership principles and strategies that transcend organizational types and models. While each industry's unique demands require unique solutions, some things are universal when leading people.

Learning the Art of Effective Leadership

One universal truth is that effective leadership is an art form. As a leader, you are an artist. Your leadership methods are your tools. Your team is your canvas. In this book, we will look at different methods and techniques you can use in creating your leadership masterpiece. Don't expect leading to happen without frustration. Be prepared to fight through some things. But remember, those things worth having are those things that are worth fighting for.

A defining moment in my journey came as a young PV2 in the US Army. Upon arrival to my duty station, my squad leader gave me a simple piece of advice. "Private Hundley," he said, "take the opportunity to learn from each leader you will have in your Army career. Whether good or bad, each leader's lessons will teach you how to be a better soldier and leader if you are willing to learn."

It's from this perspective that I have approached this book. Not wanting to simply regurgitate clichés and repackage the plethora of leadership material currently available, I seek to add my personal experience—MY lessons learned—into the mix of public discourse. Having been privileged to lead in corporate, military, and non-profit environments, I've compiled principles I believe are key to leading in any environment. These principles are helpful as we navigate this new wave of millennial workforce participants, many of whom are just entering the ranks of leadership in many organizations.

Respectfully,

Zebulan Hundley (a.k.a. Dr.Z)

2 THE LEADER IN YOU

> **Every great leader can lead in any organization, but truly great leaders refuse to lead in just any organization.**

2.1 Your Values

Those things you hold most dear define you. They define you, not only as a person but also as a leader. These things–these ideals–dictate your thoughts, your actions, and your decisions. They determine who you allow in your circle of influence and who you exclude from that circle. Yet, even with these ideals being so paramount, many people fail to even consider what their values are, let alone be intentional about selecting which values they will hold as unshakeable truths for themselves. Understanding your values takes intentional time and a willingness to look at what is real about yourself and not just what you think sounds good. Once you have taken the time to do a thorough self-examination and secure for yourself these guiding principles and ideals, you will find this clarity both strengthens you and your decision-making. This is beneficial because what you value also determines the types of organizations you will thrive in. For some, they will value honesty—even brutal honesty—above all else. Others may value loyalty in a relationship above honesty. Others may value drive and determination or the ability to turn a quick profit.

Whatever you value, know this:

What you value matters. It matters more than any other quality you will have as a leader.

If you value an easy process above all else, you will cut corners to remove the burden of process from you–even though that process is designed to both protect you and enable your success. If you value a job well done, you will often try to ensure the quality of work you do meets the highest of standards–all at the expense of your personal comfort. As a leader, if you are asked to both uphold and lead others in a pattern of behavior based on values you don't hold as your own, you will quickly see your frustration level rise and the satisfaction you receive from your efforts plummet. This pattern is not a successful one and cannot be sustained over a long period.

This is easily understood when viewed through from the perspective of a personal trainer at any local gym. Every January, gyms across the country are flooded with new applications for memberships. A vast majority of these new members are not fitness aficionados by nature. This will be evidenced by a significant decline in active participation at the gym by March. Even though these new members have signed a contract and have paid for a personal trainer to push them beyond their normal limitations, many people new to the gym don't share the value of fitness as a central driver of who they are. So, when pushed past a level of comfort they are unwilling to work with, these people quit. This is not the case with those who hold a high level of fitness near and dear to the core of their being. These individuals seem to enjoy being pushed past what is comfortable because they know that the end result is worth the temporary pain they are going through now.

As another example, many jobs in the United States Armed Forces require a degree of honesty. Those individuals who seek to work in these career fields must undergo many levels of background investigations to make sure that they are who they say they are. If someone from one of these career fields retired from their military service and became employed in an organization that encouraged dishonest practices and had low standards of honesty among the workforce, this service-member likely would not have a long and prosperous future with this new company. Once you know who you are at your core, it's difficult to work with those who would seek to change who you are to fit their agenda.

The previous examples are very much simplified, but the principle remains the same in any scenario. Those things at war with what we hold most dear are cast aside quickly for something that aligns with that which we value most.

Maybe you, like many others, have never taken the time to think about what matters most to you. Maybe you don't even know where to begin. Might I suggest that you begin by taking an inventory of where you've been? What jobs have you held that you enjoyed? What environments or leaders have you had that made you cringe? What types of entertainment are you drawn to? What do these things have in common?

Once you've identified those values that matter most to you, you are on your way to securing and branding one of the most important elements about who you are as a person. After you have had the time to assess your values, take the time to write them here:

1)_____

2)_____

3)_____

What will you NOT tolerate?

2.2 YOUR CREDIBILITY

One of the most frustrating moments in any young leader's journey comes shortly after gaining a title that tells them they are now in charge. This title acquisition is such a highly sought-after achievement by many immature leaders, but–interestingly enough–this step often brings with it more frustration than celebration once reality sets in. I say this because it's a natural assumption to think that once you are officially in charge, people will listen to you–they must, right? That sounds fine, but it's simply not the case.

Leadership is all about trust and credibility. People will not follow you if they don't trust you.

Before you gain the efforts of your team(s), you must first gain their hearts.

Trust requires a track record of performance to establish a likely pattern of behavior. This is why people trust you–they know what to expect. So, the newer you are to leading your team, the harder you must work to build this trust. This is where the values you defined in the last section will either make or break you. Did you choose values that will last, or did you choose values that favor the temporary gain at the expense of the long-term stability and return? The answer to "how do I build trust and establish credibility?" is very simple to say, but it takes time and precision to put it into action. The answer is this:

Your *yes* must be *yes* and your *no* must be *no* – <u>every time</u>.

Consistency builds credibility. Each conversation you have and each decision you make will either build or erode trust with everyone in your sphere of influence. If you make it known that you will not tolerate tardiness

Learning the Art of Effective Leadership

in the workplace, yet you are routinely late to meetings, you communicate that your preference is worth more than the plans, schedules, and tasks of everyone else in your office. This erodes trust, not only in you as a leader, but also your decision-making process. If you seem to consistently say one thing, yet do another, your pattern of behavior will show that your words cannot be trusted. If your words cannot be trusted, nothing you communicate will be trusted. If you are not trusted, you are not followed. It's that simple.

Besides making sure your words and actions are in harmony with one another, the frequency and content of your communication with those that you lead will also either build your credibility or diminish it. If you are quick to criticize and cast blame, but slow to share credit or give praise, you are eroding trust with your team—not building it. Trust creates a circle where each member of the team feels safe and valued and where there is freedom to create (and even fail) without risk of being ostracized.

Besides the frequency and content of communication, even the method you use to communicate can strategically either establish and reinforce your credibility in the workplace or sow seeds of mistrust and division. Digital communication methods like text messages make it fast and efficient to send a text for a quick response. However, it does not take many text messages received during dinner (read AFTER WORK) to erode trust that you legitimately care for the individual on your team and their total well-being. If that care and concern are doubted, anything you do as a leader to motivate your team will not be seen as motivation, but as manipulation.

Secure Your Motive

Another key to defining who you are as a leader is knowing WHY you lead in the first place. What prompted you to be in the business of shaping and developing the growth of people around you? Some of us did not choose to be in a place of leadership—it just sort of happened. Others of us chose this role. We will discuss this more in a later section, but knowing where you start is quite an important part of the map that will ultimately lead you to your destination. Until we get to that section though, it's important for you to know the answer to this question:

Do you lead because you have something to offer your team or do you lead because you want your team to do something for you?

It's easy as a leader to cast vision around OUR thoughts, ideas, and plans. It's easy to understand the benefits of our thought-out strategies and procedures. It's exciting as a leader to look at the potential victories and profits of our effort and it's difficult to understand when those who report to us don't share in our enthusiasm. In this book, we will give practical steps you can take to win buy-in from your team and how to lead them into fulfilling your vision. However, before you get too excited about your plans to conquer your world, understand this:

> **If you want buy-in FROM them,
> you first must buy INTO them.**

It has often been said that people don't care what you know until they know that you care. This is true and is one place where your leadership's credibility has the potential to pay significant dividends if you have established your track record properly. In these chapters, we will explore this process of buy-in in more detail, but a crucial element to establishing your credibility is establishing your visibility.

As a leader, if you are not visible, you are not valuable.

This visibility I am referencing is not the exciting visibility of a stage or television broadcast. This is not the kind of visibility that would make for a very good television show or poignant moment captured by today's ratings-driven media. This visibility is the behind-the-scenes, "boots-on-the-ground" type of visibility that lets those you lead know that you are in the fight with them.

The facility walk-through at six o'clock in the morning—long before the average person cares to be awake (let alone functioning)—to let the sanitation crew know that they are appreciated is worth much more—when establishing your credibility as a leader—than the interview with the local news station at six o'clock that evening ever will. The meeting where you allow your subordinates to lead (while you give the living example of how to follow and contribute to the mission of those above you) speaks more about how others should follow you than any rule book or policy document could ever do.

This visibility shows the "average worker" that they are more than average to you. It shows you value ALL employees and that EVERYTHING and EVERYONE under your sphere of influence matters to you. If your track record values others, leads by example, and places the well-being of your team above your own, then gaining buy-in from your team will not be a difficult task. However, the opposite is also true.

If your reputation states you have neither the time, nor the inclination to be bothered with those things that do not immediately draw attention to yourself, or if your reputation states you will quickly allow others to be the scapegoat to ensure that you get the credit, then you will be hard-pressed to win over any skeptics or get even a little buy-in from your team when presenting a new idea or set of plans you wish them to carry out. The perceived value of your ideas will always be skewed by the assumption that your plans only look out for YOUR best interest–not OUR best interest.

This is a critical point because as leaders we are charged with taking people beyond their comfort zones and into uncharted territory to achieve things as a team that would otherwise be impossible. If your credibility as a leader is high, your team will hear your vision and see your implementation plan as something motivating, exciting, and full of potential. If your credibility is low, those same motivational words will be seen not as motivation, but as manipulation.

> To be persuasive, we must be believable;
>
> to be believable, we must be credible;
>
> to be credible, we must be truthful.
>
> –Edward R. Murrow

2.3 KEY QUESTIONS

1) What are the core values that define your leadership?

2) What is your reputation in your organization?

3) What would you like to change about that reputation?

4) What steps will you take to change your reputation?

3 Your Destination

I am fairly certain that most of us–if not all–have had the "privilege" of working under a leader that seemed to have no idea where they were going or what they were doing. Decisions (no matter how important) seemed based on knee-jerk reactions and a distorted view of reality that only they saw. For the team underneath this leader, the workday was filled with activity, but it never felt like anything was actually accomplished.

Think back to a time where you were under that type of a leader. What was the morale in the workplace like? How much confidence did the team members have in their leader? What was the nature of the relationships in the workplace? Was your workplace simply a place of employment or was it something you could enjoy pouring yourself into?

As leaders, we must understand how vital it is that we know what we are trying to accomplish.

We must know why we exist as leaders in that specific organization. If we don't know that for ourselves, how can we expect those team members under our umbrella of influence to know what they are there for? And if they don't know what we are trying to accomplish together, then they will not achieve the consistent results needed to build the momentum that will carry the team to its destination successfully.

So, after you know who you are as a leader, the next step in this journey of leadership is to define where you will lead your team. For example, a family who says they are planning a vacation was asked where they are going. "To the beach," they said. This idea sounds nice, but which beach are they going to?

> *"And the Lord answered me: "Write the vision; make it plain on tablets, so he may run who reads it." —Habakkuk 2:2*

If you want to arrive at your destination together as a team, each team member *must* understand—with specific detail—where you are going. If instead of saying you were going to the beach, you said that you were going to a beach on the Gulf of Mexico, I would say you are getting better at communicating. If you said that you were going to meet at a particular restaurant on Anna Maria Island, Florida—about fifty miles south of Tampa, I would say you are doing a great job in determining your destination and communicating it in such a way that the others you want to join you are likely to actually arrive with you.

When defining your destination to your team members, there is another element to consider.

Is your destination worth the cost it will require to get there?

If someone offered you a once-in-a-lifetime opportunity to fly in a new state-of-the-art airplane for only one thousand dollars, you might get excited. But if the destination of that airplane was only a fifteen-minute drive from the launch site, would you pay that fee? Likely you would not.

Unless it was a life-long dream of yours to fly in that aircraft, many people would not have the luxury of spending one thousand dollars on a fifteen-minute excursion. Whether we like to think this way or not, a natural response to any new venture–no matter how grand or noble–that we must anticipate and mitigate is the age-old question: "What's in it for me?"

So, if the destination you are communicating to your team is simply meeting your daily sales goals, dream bigger. What is something that your team members can latch onto, take ownership of, and wear as a badge of honor? What opportunity are you offering your team to be a part of something larger than themselves? If your store had the reputation as the top-selling store in the entire corporate family–resulting in the highest bonuses paid to its employees–wouldn't that make the daily grind in the office seem much more worth it to your team members on those cold and rainy days when they otherwise would rather stay home? If your destination doesn't have real value to each member of the team, then the team won't have a desire to reach it with you.

However, where are you going with your team? Write your plainly-written destination below.

_____

_____

_____

Now that the destination has been put into writing, is it something that is plainly written and easily understood, or is it written in language or terminology that only you can understand? If the destination is not written in verbiage that everyone on your team—from the newest member to the most mature veteran—can understand, it must be rewritten. Take the time to get this right. If you feel this step is a waste of your time, please understand that the purpose of a leader is not simply to get stuff done, but instead to help everyone arrive together as you are getting stuff done. If that is not a primary concern, I would advise you to go back and review earlier pages in this book and check your motive.

Remember this:

If you want your team to buy into your vision, you must first buy into them.

Learning the Art of Effective Leadership

If they don't trust you are leading them to something that is in their best interest, simply having a clearly-defined destination will never be enough.

Now, let's say that your destination has been defined and it's plainly written so that all can understand it. That's a great step and it's a key step in any leadership role you will ever have. You have also gone through a self-examination and you know that your motive is pure and that your team is bought into you as their leader. Now you have the task of communicating this destination to your team.

You are a leader, in part, because you see things before others do. This enables you to find solutions that others cannot find. You seem to do on accident what many other people fail to do on purpose. You cannot even always explain it, you just know how to see steps beyond your current challenge. Sometimes it's easy to forget that others don't see what you do. But think about it for a moment. If they did, why would they need you to lead them? Don't fall into frustration because others on your team don't seem to "get it."

You might see BEFORE them, but you cannot see FOR them.

So how do you help them see? The answer isn't found in simply repeating the same verbiage repeatedly. Not that having a unified verbiage is not valuable, but if that was the answer leading would be easy–at least much easier than it really is. It is not found in punitive measures based on a failure to reach goals that the team does not understand. It's much simpler than that.

You help the team see by communicating the destination clearly and often. When communicating the destination, you must clearly communicate not only the "where" of the destination but the "why" behind it. Why is THIS destination the right destination? Once you have clearly defined the "where" and the "why" behind your destination and you have buy-in from your team, now is the time to plan the "how."

3.1 CHART THE COURSE

> "Vision without execution is hallucination." – Henry Ford

Creating the Action Plan

Decisions made in a vacuum are always bound for trouble. By that, I mean it's easy as a leader to think you know what is best for your vision and to chart a course based on your understanding of how things *should* work. This is especially true when you don't include the input from knowledgeable people with the ability to provide insight that would improve your plan. The trouble with that approach is that things don't always work like we think they should. As individuals, we automatically have a limited view of any situation or scenario. We have blind spots created by ignorance, ego, and lack of experience. So how do you gain a real understanding of the day-to-day impact of your decision making to ensure you have the best plan moving forward? You start by getting feedback from those who would directly feel the impacts of your plan.

I've found there are two circles I include at two key times when determining a strategic approach to get where we are wanting to go. The first circle is large. It includes a pre-determined sample of the people or departments involved in implementing a particular set of plans. This circle brainstorms new ideas, poking holes in the existing proposed courses of action, and suggesting improvement from each team's perspective. From this setting I can gather key pieces of information such as the level of buy-in from this group and the teams they represent, a better understanding of key obstacles in the proposed set of plans that must be addressed before rollout, and many opinions and personalities that will prove very valuable when looking at which team I want to put together for the next circle.

The second circle is much smaller–

necessarily so.

The first circle brings creativity, ideas, and a general pulse of the organization on the proposed direction for the effort. The second circle is a decision-making circle. This is the group that will have a heavy influence on the final set of plans and will be the primary champions of the vision and implementation of that vision once it's time to put these plans into action. Generally, key influencers from the first circle will find themselves in the second circle. This is an important part of getting buy-in from the group. The more these influencers can feel like they are a part of the process, the more they will own the process. The more that they own the process, the more they will champion it for you. This snowballs into a much greater excitement about the path ahead and makes the rollout of your implementation plans much easier.

Learning the Art of Effective Leadership

In each circle, your job as the leader is to provide general vision, and then let the team take the lead on generating ideas. The more you share your own ideas in meetings with these circles, the less sharing will take place. The natural tendency of team members is to default to the leader, so by holding your own tongue and sharing your own ideas last, you communicate value to the team you are assembling, and you are showing an openness to their ideas and opinions.

In each setting, as the leader, you will be the one charged with championing the vision and making sure that any proposals are focused on keeping the "main thing" the "main thing." In this process, you must undoubtedly address doubts and uncertainties about the plausibility of the end goal. Don't take these doubts personally. Remember that you have had much longer to think through this idea than your team has. If you hit an impasse, now is your time to step in and shine—not by giving them your grand plan, but by helping them to see the next step. This teaches the team not just *what* to think, but it helps them to learn *how* to think.

> **Help them achieve the impossible by showing them what IS possible.**

Setting goals

No matter how grand your vision is, you should not expect people on your teams to achieve it without having a defined path set out before them. This path should be well-marked and have plenty of opportunities for both evaluation and celebration. This is a key to building momentum for your team. In a game of American football, momentum is not achieved only after a game has been won. Momentum is achieved when play after play is executed well and the ball is consistently moved toward the end zone. Each successful play builds confidence in the leadership, the team, and the plan. The opposite is also true. A failure to consistently execute successful plays will destroy both momentum and morale.

With this in mind, you must set goals for your team so the team knows that it's doing well and that the plan is putting them on a path to success. A well-defined goal (score a touchdown) without a defined path (game plan) leads to frustration as the team's excitement dwindles with each mistake. A well-defined path (game plan) without a well-defined goal (score a touchdown) is exhausting as there seems to be no point to the energy exertion. But when a well-defined path leads to a well-defined goal and it's consistently executed and celebrated, magic happens. Motivation, trust, and effort all run at high levels and the result is a highly energetic and productive experience.

When setting goals for your team, a few things must be true for these goals to produce the consistent momentum to further your organization. Without these, your mission will be much harder to complete, and your results will likely be inconsistent and unreliable. Don't be lazy in goal-setting. If you want your team's best, give the team your best.

These goals must:

- Be attainable
- Be measurable
- Be repeatable

- Be completed by a certain time
- Be connected to the "why"

Attainable

Not much will frustrate your team like consistently setting unrealistic goals. While a lack of having goals is frustrating, unrealistic goals basically say that you have no real goals—all while pretending you do. Consistently over-inflating what you say you want your team to achieve is not motivating. That is worth repeating again.

Consistently over-inflating what you say you want your team to achieve IS NOT MOTIVATING.

The opposite is true. If, as a leader, you are known for setting impossible goals, the team will have no motivation to try to reach those goals. When setting goals for your team, you want these goals to be just barely outside of the team's reach. Goals too easy to reach are not goals, they are expectations. Goals just outside of the reach of normalcy will motivate your team to accomplish something beyond what they normally would do and will give the team something to celebrate once the goal has been reached. Remember, anything that is worth celebrating is worth fighting for.

Measurable

These goals also must be measurable. You cannot change what you don't track, and you cannot track what cannot be measured. It's not enough to simply tell your employees that their goal for the day is to make their client's day better. How will you know whether that was achieved? What mechanism will you use to measure it? If your team will not do what you expect unless you take the time to inspect it, how will the team know whether their performance has measured up to the expected standard unless you give them the expected standard? It sounds obvious, but this element is often overlooked.

Repeatable

Growth is not measured by what you do on accident during a one-time spike in performance, but rather by what you consistently do in practice. Setting a personal peak performance point is fun, but consistently performing at a higher level—and tracking that performance—is where the sweet spot lies. If you can replicate the same result repeatedly, you are now performing at a higher level and you are ready to stretch further. Repeating this goal-setting process–stretch, attain, maintain–will cause a situation where your old ceiling (what was just out of reach) is now your floor (what you are using as a platform to advance to the next level).

Deadlines

If we are honest, people are motivated by two things – "want to" and "have to." Unless your team is a highly motivated group of self-starters, they are unlikely to complete achieving these out-of-reach goals within a timeline that will produce consistent momentum. This is where you, as a leader, have to set the team's pace. If you can keep them moving forward, then the goals will be met and the celebration will commence. This will build momentum and will give your team the motivational fuel it needs to meet the next challenge.

Think about deadlines as if they were the bank to a river. Water without the restricting banks around it becomes a stagnant pool that produces a lot of smell and is of little value. With banks, however, this same water now moves with a current and can power entire cities with hydro-electric energy. Without the structure of deadlines, your team will likely grow stagnant (though hopefully without the stink). If you want to keep your team moving forward, establish a timeline and include that in the definition of the goal's success.

Connection to the "why"

The goals set for your team also must have an obvious purpose that connects to the "why." It's easy for team members to forget the big picture. As the leader, you must connect your team to the larger vision that fuels the tasks. Constantly communicate the importance of an individual task to completing the mission. If you as a leader cannot identify why you are doing something, then why ARE you doing it?

Path to the Destination

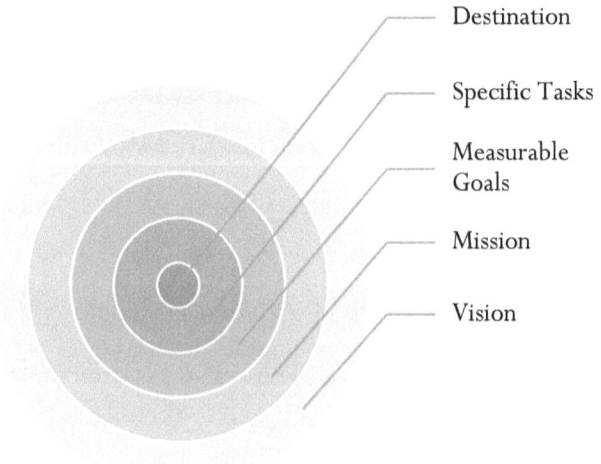

3.2 LAUNCH A NEW INITIATIVE

The Pre-Launch

Casting Vision

Perhaps the most important part of launching a new initiative is developing, refining, and properly communicating your vision for this new initiative. Whether you are leading a product launch, rebranding effort, launching a new startup business or creating a non-profit organization, the vision behind the effort is what will ultimately connect your team to its purpose.

Without purpose, minimum effort will be given, and mediocrity will be the accepted result.

However, if a team is both connected to, and united behind, a common vision and they know "why" they are working so hard and "who" will benefit from their creativity and innovation, a standard of excellence will not be merely tolerated, but will become a badge of honor. What can be tricky, though, is knowing who needs to understand what part of the vision and when.

The simple reality that all leaders must understand is that everyone does not want them to succeed. It's easy enough to understand that your competitors would want you to falter, but often, others in your own organization will not want your vision to succeed. This should not prompt you to view everyone through the lens of paranoia but should encourage you to take a measured approach when sharing new ideas.

The care you take in communicating this information now will determine the level of repair you must make later.

So, how do we determine Who must know What, and When they must know that information?

First, start by sharing these plans with your closest and most trusted advisors. Let them help you poke holes in the idea and refine your message. Once each advisor is fully on board with the idea, you then slowly expand your circle and take your vision to a small group of key decision-makers. These top-level decision makers will be the ones in charge of both communicating and implementing the nuts-and-bolts of the vision in their department. It's both courteous and wise to allow them to ask questions and get behind the vision before going any further.

Once your trusted advisors and key decision-makers understand and support this vision, you then take this vision to those next in line to be affected by this vision before presenting publicly. Communicating in this order shows your team you value them enough to keep them informed, but also to empower them with the correct information so they are not caught off-guard if approached with a question about supposed change in the air. When you empower your team with the right information, you are all stronger.

As a practical example, we can point to something as simple as a church adding another opportunity for worship during the week. The pastor might be convinced this is the right move, but if the pastor announces on their personal social media page that a new service is being added before ever talking with other leaders in the church who would run various aspects of this event, one can easily see how this error in communication can cause confusion and a breakdown in trust between leaders.

A better way of communicating this change would be for the pastor to first speak with key staff so they can prepare their departments for any needed logistical shifts for this expanded service. After the staff was both aware and prepared, the pastor could then approach key volunteers and inform them of the upcoming change to keep them both informed and excited about the new opportunities for growth. Once these key volunteers have been notified, then announcing to the church during a regularly scheduled service, and then to the public through social media and other avenues would ensure that all leaders in the organization feel valued and can join in the celebration of the launch rather than dreading something that was thrust upon them.

Learning the Art of Effective Leadership

Now that we have a better understanding of the correct order in which we should communicate, we should explore another important aspect of communicating vision. Every person—even every leader—need not have access to the same level of information. The end goal when casting vision is to both inform and inspire, but each set of leaders needs a different mix of information and inspiration to stay properly engaged in implementing the vision.

Continuing with our earlier example of the pastor communicating an additional worship offering, when you speak with your most trusted advisors, cast a "big picture" vision. This is not the time for mind-numbing, granular details. When communicating with key staff, details must answer the logistical questions, and this will obtain their buy-in. When moving on to key volunteers, add *some* details, but keep mostly to a "big picture" perspective. They don't need the same granular detail that your key staff requires at this stage.

> **As a general rule, the larger the crowd you are communicating with, the fewer the details needed.**

Additional details prompt additional questions and larger audiences are not the ideal environment for fielding and answering these questions. Taking the proper time to analyze, refine, and properly communicate your vision will eliminate unnecessary confusion, increase buy-in and excitement, and will create a healthy momentum in your organization as you prepare for your launch. But before you are ready to pull the trigger and begin the implementation, you should run systems checks to ensure you have the needed systems and structures in place to not only attain success in reaching your end goal but to sustain success once you reach it.

Having the right systems and structures

> **System:** a regularly interacting or interdependent group of items forming a unified whole.

Every organization comprises systems and structures. They are how the organization gets things done. If you perform an action one time, it's an action. If you perform the action a second time, it's now part of a system. Systems can either be very complex, or they can be very simple. They can also come in a variety of forms. But be sure of this, even an organization governed by no formal system is still operating under a system.

The question is not whether or not a system exists in your organization. The question is whether your system is effective in achieving your stated goals. Will your system sustain your success or sabotage it? The strength and depth of your systems and structures will determine the heights at which your organization will reside.

Your organization can achieve great heights without strong support systems, but it cannot reside there.

For example, let us say you are preparing to launch a new product. A prototype has been created and through savvy use of social media, the world is in awe of your masterpiece. You take orders for your product before you can mass-produce that product. Due to the viral nature of social media, your product now has gained worldwide attention. This is exciting, but you quickly realize it's getting beyond what you can do.

Orders pour in from all over the globe. Because your support systems are not in place, you cannot fulfill these orders. The demand is so overwhelming, you cannot keep up with the orders received. You now have many angry customers that use the viral nature of social media to dissuade potential customers from purchasing your product. Your amazing product is now widely viewed as a scam and consumer trust in you is broken.

The above simplified example highlights the importance of making sure that the right systems are in place before attempting to implement your vision. Each organization will have different needs and requirements, so we will not be going in depth about any particular system here, but failing to mention the importance of having the systems in place would be a great disservice to the leader learning to do things thoroughly and with excellence.

Some key questions (but not all of them) to ask in determining whether or not your systems are in place and ready for the launch are this:

- How will we communicate internally?
- How will we communicate to the customer?
- How will we ensure quality and consistency?
- What data do we need to collect?

- How will we keep track of that important data?
- How will we measure success or failure?
- Will any additional personnel or equipment be needed for this system to operate?
- Are all team members proficient in these systems and processes or will additional training be required?
- Who has decision making authority and how will we let that information be known?
- How will we develop the future leadership for the long-term success of these systems and structures?

Once you have identified which systems must be in place now, you will want to look at them through another lens.

Will these systems support me for what is next?

I would urge any leader to not be content with temporary, bandage-type solutions. Always think in the "what is now/what is next" mindset. To add consistency and predictability–think stability–to your launch, you don't want to outgrow your current systems just as your team is becoming proficient in them. Once you are sure the right systems are in place for both what is needed now and what will be needed in the next phase of operation, the next step is determining which people must be in which position to ensure these systems are running smoothly.

If we were talking about a vehicle with a dead battery, that vehicle's system would need a new battery to replace the old one. If you put a carburetor in place of the old battery, you would not get the vehicle to function as it was designed to function. For the system to work properly, the system needs the correct part in correct place. Otherwise, the system may be full of parts great at what they do, but assembled as they are they cannot accomplish anything. The same is true when seeking leaders to fill positions in your system.

I've been a part of many institutions that placed a higher priority on seniority than it did on whether that individual was the right person for a particular role in the system. This culture leads to an environment where many great people exist, but motivation and productivity are low because of the right people being in the wrong position. This is especially dangerous because the success or failure of any organization or effort depends completely on the leadership within it. It's always easier to promote a leader than it is to demote a leader, so rather than being content to find a person and try to fit them into a role, I propose a different approach.

The approach I use is to clearly define a role, its expectations, its requirements, and the capacity to fulfill that role. Once that has been identified, I find a leader specifically created for that role. This is a much easier process in organizations with a strong sense of identity and a culture of leadership development very intentional about building the leaders it needs. If you are not in such an organization, all is not lost. You will just have more work ahead of you as you build that culture. Sometimes these leaders will be in your existing leadership teams, but often they are not. I would encourage you to not take shortcuts in this decision-making process. The very existence of your vision depends on the right leaders, so deliberate with caution.

Once you have found the right fit, then make that decision firmly and with confidence. Ensure clarity among your team so each team member knows who is responsible for what and who has the authority to do what. Do this and you are well on your way to a successful launch.

Capacity

A brief thought on having leaders with the right capacity in the right positions in your systems. Not all leaders are created equally. It's easy to quickly identify someone gifted at accomplishing a task and to be tempted to put them in a position of leadership because of their gifting. Having a gifted leader helps, but there's a big difference between being a great salesperson and leading a team of salespeople. A wise leader will focus more on a candidate's capacity to lead a team more than their ability to complete a task.

Implementing the Plan

You have identified yourself as a leader, you know that your motivation is pure, you have solidified your vision, communicated it properly, you have mapped out a plan, and have identified key leaders for key elements of your system. That is a lot of work! Take a moment to sit back and reflect on this part of the journey. Celebrate (if you have not already) and breathe deeply. The hard work is about to begin.

Hopefully, you are not like most leaders. Most leaders try to do the above by themselves. It's not until they question their existence and success as a leader that they learn about this amazing opportunity to get more done at a faster rate and with much more enjoyment. This opportunity is called empowerment.

You cannot do this alone.

If the height you can both attain and sustain rests on the strength of the systems and hinges on the leadership within it, there has to be more in that leadership circle than just you. Unfortunately, many leaders surround themselves with very capable leaders but don't empower them to lead. This leads to much higher overhead cost, much higher frustration on the team, and one very exhausted leader who does not understand why everything seems so hard. If you only take one thing away from this book, let it be this.

As a leader, you exist to empower other leaders.

Much noise has been made about the importance of delegation. I would agree that delegation is important, but not as important as empowerment. Though very much connected, they are different. It's very similar to facial tissue. Every Kleenex is a facial tissue, but not every facial tissue is a Kleenex. Similarly, all empowerment involves delegation, but not all delegation is empowerment. So, how do you know the difference between the two?

The first major difference between delegation and empowerment is the direction in which they flow. Delegation flows from the top to the bottom. A manager may divide tasks and will assign different tasks to different people. The team has only the authority to do what was on the task list–nothing more and nothing less. Because the manager retains all decision-making authority, each time an issue or question arises about the task list, the manager must provide the answer. This makes the manager feel important and solidifies their role as the subject-matter expert in all areas of the business. This also hamstrings the manager because they are never free to focus on other items that only they can do as they are frequently tied up with these other matters.

Conversely, empowerment starts at the top and flows to the bottom, but then also flows from the bottom back up to the top. This creates a 360-degree loop of empowerment that enables each member to be both efficient and effective. When empowerment happens in a similar scenario, a manager involves his team in dividing up the tasks, so each member knows their role and the role of every other member of the team. Each member is then given a certain and known amount of authority to decide within their area of responsibility, leaving only the highest level of decision-making to the manager. With each team member knowing their responsibility and authority, everyone goes out to fulfill their assigned roles.

The manager, now freed up from having to make every decision, is now free to focus on leading in areas where other team members don't have insight and are only distracted if a serious issue arises. When true empowerment happens, a culture of trust is solidified, and each team member knows their role, their authority, and it frees them up to focus only on that. If you are not sure whether you have been delegating or empowering, consider this question. Would you say that your regular pattern of behavior is handing out your plans for others to carry out, or do you allow others to help craft these plans?

Empowerment lets others in on creating the plans.

This develops a sense of ownership and pride in the plans and allows a more knowledgeable and focused leader to fulfill their area(s) of responsibility. Another key component of empowerment is ensuring those under your leadership have the tools and resources required to fulfill their responsibilities. Nothing is more frustrating as an employee than being asked to fulfill a role or complete a task without having the resources to accomplish the mission. This is especially true if that employee is not given the authority to operate with freedom as they seek to acquire those resources.

In some circles, these resources are called the beans and bullets. Imagine for a moment you are about to embark on a military campaign. You are given the task of capturing a particular tower in a city. You know that the enemy is deeply entrenched. What are the things you would need to know to be able to craft a plan of attack?

You wouldn't likely try to accomplish this task without the help and assistance of others, so knowing who is available, what their skill sets are, what ammunition is at your disposal, the known locations of the enemy troops and other key information is essential in planning and coordinating a successful mission. Sharing essential information helps everyone on the team. If you hoard information so you can be the only repository for correct answers, you are not empowering your team for success. In the near-term, this may seem like a great strategy for gaining your own promotion, but long-term, this trait—if not abandoned—will only limit your ability to lead at high levels.

Information-sharing cannot happen without trust, but blind trust is dangerous. As a leader, your role is not just to accomplish tasks, but to protect the organization in which you lead. Part of the systems and structures you must have in place is a mechanism to ensure accountability. This is easily seen in the financial realm where each corporate purchase requires a receipt to prove where the company's resources were used. This accountability system strengthens trust within the organization and enables leaders to empower employees with the authority to purchase approved items without the management having to make every purchase themselves. This same principle applies to each area.

Whether it's data collection, setting and meeting deadlines, sales quotas, or new customer leads, without accountability, your goals are very unlikely to be met. Accountability keeps the focus on the most important thing. Those you lead will not do what you expect of them, they will only consistently do what you inspect. What you take time to inspect communicates what is important to you as a leader.

Standards without accountability aren't standards.

Clear communication is essential to ensuring that empowerment is not a fleeting thought, but a long-standing pillar in the culture of your organization. Encouraging and actively seeking feedback on the pulse of the organization, morale, efficiency, effectiveness, and leadership will only strengthen the teams you lead. Conversely, a failure to communicate with those on your team will cultivate an environment of distrust, assumption, and unproductive activity. Few things are worse than an organization full of activity but accomplishing nothing. Communication is what will keep your teams focused on the vision and is what will ensure that the mission's objectives are clear.

A wise leader will build into their systems a way to ensure two-way communication occurs with regularity and that real, accurate feedback is received at the appropriate times. Part of this system of communication should focus on periodic reviews of the organization, effort, etc. and focuses not only on the positive or fun aspects of the discussion. Wise leaders don't fear knowing what is good, what is bad, and what is ugly (GBUs).

GBUs show us what to continue and where to improve. I recommend any leader makes GBUs a central focus of any event recap. Highlighting what succeeded gives the team something to celebrate, and what you reward will be repeated. Highlighting what failed and needs improvement is critical to growth and long-term success. This should not be a time where fingers are pointed at people. This should solely be focused on pointing out issues or flaws in the system used.

It's easy to point fingers and blame an individual, but what went wrong in the system that didn't catch the individual's mistake? People are not perfect, and they will always make mistakes, so you should use this time to strengthen your accountability systems to mitigate these impending missteps. Clearly evaluating each milestone or major step of the launch will only add to the success of the launch you are undertaking.

In evaluating the GBUs, you will undoubtedly identify an area of concern that, if left unchanged, could be disastrous. So, what do you do when that area of concern is found? Once an area of concern has been identified you can shore up an area of your system if it has not already been put into place.

This portion of the book has focused on elements critical to empowering those that you lead. This is yet another piece of that puzzle. Once you have identified this area of concern, bring it to the attention of your key team leaders. As leaders, we are never content to simply announce a problem, we are solution-minded, so involve your team in identifying a solution.

When you break from this meeting with your key leaders, these questions should be answered:

- What element of the system needs to be changed?

- How soon must this change occur?

- What is the deadline for a solution to be found?

- Who makes the final decision on what solution will be implemented?

- What notification procedures must be in place to alert each person involved?

Once the final systems checks have been completed, all final changes have been made, and each person on every team knows that each other team is ready to launch, NOW is the time to execute your dream!

Celebrating the Launch

The day has finally arrived. All of your hard work (your blood, your sweat, and your tears) has finally manifested in this day–launch day. Don't let this launch happen without a celebration. It's not merely another day. Your launch event is not simply another event. This event has great importance and should be celebrated. Take time—intentional time—to recognize your team members and let them join in this celebration. Be quick to share credit and allow your team to own this victory. The celebration need not be anything expensive or implemented on a grand scale but don't underestimate the importance of gratitude for your team in this process. Remember, they will repeat what you reward.

How you handle this roll-out will have a significant impact on the level of buy-in for your next launch, so be generous with thanks and reserve any criticism for another time. If the team feels used and abused after this launch, you will have a very tough time generating excitement around the next step in the vision.

3.3 Make the Journey

Now that the launch has happened, it's time to put your support systems to the test. It takes a lot of energy and effort to get a new idea or project off of the ground, but it takes intentional effort to continue the climb to success and maintain that success once it arrives. This is not the time to sit back and relax. You had your opportunity to do that during the launch celebration. Tomorrow's success depends on you not putting today's success on a permanent platform. Now is the time to get to work checking systems, collecting and interpreting data, developing your leaders, and leading your team to the next destination. As you do so, don't forget the steps you took to get to this point. Each step is critically important to your continued success, so don't neglect them now!

Learning the Art of Effective Leadership

With the launch behind you, many of your team members have likely been consumed by the daily tasks needed to realize that launch. A launch is new and exciting. Maintaining the systems to ensure future stability and growth is much less exciting. Once the newness has worn off, what was once exciting can become mundane. What was once celebrated, now becomes the expected norm. Be intentional about reconnecting your team to the original vision. Failure to keep the vision at the forefront of all you do can cause a significant loss of momentum following the launch. If that happens, much of the energy you spent doing things right the first time is wasted. It's much better to keep progressing. A moving car is much easier to turn in another direction than one sitting still.

Visibility

Some things can be done daily to keep the vision in front of your team. The first, and most important, steps that can be taken are the daily steps you take in front of your team. Never underestimate the power of your presence.

As a leader, you are not valuable if you are not visible.

Too many leaders are content to sit in a back office somewhere. There they analyze charts, interpret data, and make decisions that directly affect the welfare of each member of the organization. When times are good, this can be tolerated, but the error of this thinking is shown as soon as some difficulties or crisis arises. If the leader appears to be disengaged from the vision and out of touch with the rank and file members in the organization, mistrust will manifest at the most crucial moment when unity is needed. Staying connected to the lives of those under your leadership is a crucial part of maintaining this unity.

President George W. Bush received a harsh lesson in this reality once photographs of him surfaced after the devastating Hurricane Katrina. These photographs did not show the President on the ground with his hands dirty–helping those that were in dire need. The photographs released to, and by, the media were of him sitting comfortably in Air Force One, calmly and comfortably surveying the damage from many feet up in the air–safe, secure, and secluded.

This one moment did not define the totality of his thoughts or feelings about those affected by the destructive force of nature, but the reality did not matter as much as the perception of reality did. When difficult times arise, people get hurt… and hurt people hurt people. The care you take to be visibly involved in your vision and in the teams of those carrying it out will determine the repair you must make if any difficulty or crisis arises.

This daily involvement–not in the minute details of daily operations, but in a visible role–of carrying out the organization's vision also gives much latitude when it's time to have a course correction. Sometimes, the correction is a system change like was earlier discussed. Sometimes though, the correction is in the behavior or mindset of an individual. If this person trusts you as a leader and trusts you lead by example–not asking of others what you are unwilling to do yourself, then they are more likely to be receptive to constructive criticism, correction, and transition. Trust is the foundation of leadership, and if you try to take the easy and convenient route now, that trust will be unlikely to exist when and where you need it.

Thinking Ahead

So, you have arrived.... now what? As a leader, it's never okay to delegate thinking about the future to someone else. Think of yourself as an airline pilot. You have many passengers on board. Each passenger has their own purpose and agenda. Each of you on board is headed to the same destination, yet each passenger cannot see what you see from the cockpit. The passengers can understand where they are headed but they can only see where they have been. Only you can see where you are going with complete clarity. You see the storms before they approach, and you adjust. You see the mountains that must be avoided and the view of the beach that the other passengers would love to have a glimpse of as they pass by. Now, with this in mind, what would happen if you emptied the fuel reserves?

The airplane designed for flight would lose momentum and would cease to move forward at the appropriate rate–resulting in a very tumultuous ride as the pilot was now forced to consider "what's next." As a leader, any time you are not actively in the pilot's seat – anticipating what is next, you are dumping your fuel reserves into thin air. The organization you lead depends on you for direction and oversight.

If you don't think about what is ahead,

who will?

This is why continued empowerment is so critical to the long-term success of your organization. If, as a leader, you get bogged down in the minute details of everyone else's duties, you are not focused on the path ahead. The higher up you are on the organizational chart, the less time you should spend being focused on today and the more time you should spend being focused on the future. What that means, is that when prioritizing your weekly schedule, don't make the same mistake I did for many years.

Don't be content to prioritize the schedule that others set for you. Instead, schedule your priorities *FIRST* and then add other things only as they are needed. This will help you focus on keeping the vision a priority in your day to day schedule.

Many leaders like to think that they are leading out of vision, but their schedule shows they are not leading out of vision, but out of crisis suppression.

This is a breakdown of my average week:

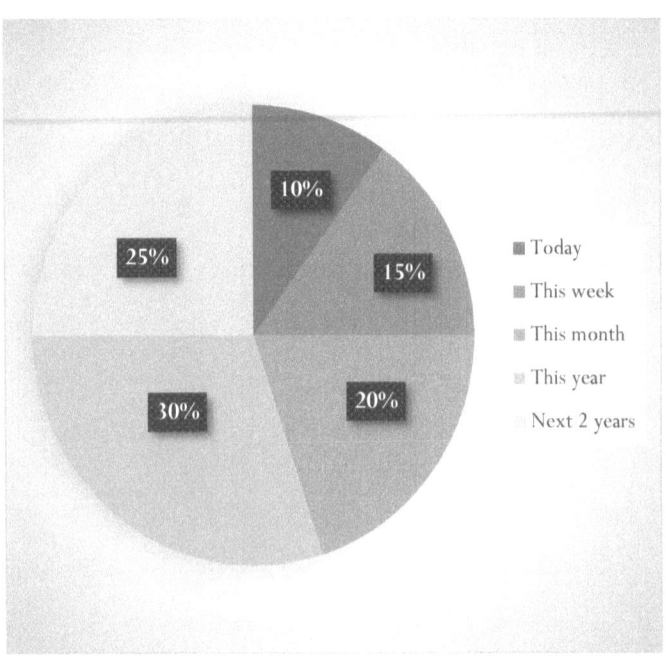

Transition

This truth cannot be overstated.

> **As a leader, if you are not planning for transition to occur on your team, you are wrong.**

It has often been said that if you fail to plan, you plan to fail. This is no truer than it is when dealing with transition on your team. Transition is inevitable. People move, plans change, and unforeseen circumstances present themselves at the most inopportune moments. When leading in your organization, you will have transition plans in place. If you have never thought about what would happen if some of your key members were taken out of the loop, now is the time to do so.

Imagine for a moment what would happen if your most-valued team member suddenly could not continue working on your team. Who would take their place? Is there anyone qualified? If not, you have just identified a crucial area for improvement. It would be well worth the time and effort to invest in finding and training the right candidates for that potential outcome. It would be wise to have leaders at every level in your organization thinking this way. Make this thought process a central part of the leadership culture on your team.

Long-term stability and continuity in an organization depend on the leadership pipeline in place. More so than any other investment an organization can make, investing in the leadership team will have the greatest return on your investment. The time and money you spend helping to develop empowered leaders that know not just "what" to think, but also "how" to think will manifest through wise decision making and intelligent risk-taking.

Keeping "what is next" in front of you will help to keep you both alert to and aware of the changing conditions that will affect your organization's performance. This is true in each area–not just personnel. Technology advances at a ridiculous pace. We know of this for purchasing a cell phone, but most leaders don't stop to think that their products and services might one day be obsolete.

Great leaders are always moving toward the next thing. Not that they are unhappy with the current status of things, it's just that these leaders realize that greater things lie ahead. The challenge is not necessarily in seeing further as a leader; the challenge is knowing when to breathe, when to move forward, and how you maintain excellence in what you are doing now, while also focusing your leadership team on what is coming.

Succession

This is also true as it applies to your role as a leader in your organization. You are not a leader because you only look out for yourself, but because others realize that you see what they do not. There's something about you that understands the need to anticipate challenges that others cannot imagine, let alone see them and plan for them. This venture started with you. Your dreams. Your investment. Your sleepless nights. What is the final destination of this vision? Is it supposed to die with you or carry on beyond your years?

Unless you intend on your team packing up and going home on the day you cannot continue–allowing everything you built to grind to a halt, you should be planning for your own "what is next."

However, many team members have sacrificed their time, energy, and treasure to help you achieve your place in leadership. The least you can do for them is to have a plan in place, with leaders you have developed that are ready to step up and fulfill the rights and responsibilities of your role.

Each of your senior team members should understand the general plan of action now to avoid confusion and conflict later. This does not need to be a part of the daily discussion, but these plans certainly must be known and understood to provide as much stability and continuity as possible during a transition that is as difficult as your departure might be. Ideally, your systems and structures are strong enough and you have empowered your team well enough that the mission will continue running on all cylinders while the existing leadership processes and enacts the needed steps to ensure a successful transition from one leader to another.

These steps are often overlooked by non-profit organizations in most dire need of these plans. Relying heavily on donations and volunteerism, many non-profits operate from a personality-driven perspective rather than from a healthy systems perspective. It's crucial that a succession plan is in place for these organizations.

3.4 Key Questions

What is the succession plan for your role in the organization?

Who should you be training and empowering to lead at the next level?

What exposure or experience does this person need to fill your shoes and move the organization forward in your absence?

4 YOUR STARTING POINT

So, you have read this far and now you are ready to jump into the proverbial water with both feet. Well, just like a GPS must know your starting point before it can point you in the right direction, it's important for you as a leader to know where you are starting from to know how to best lead others to your destination. In this section, we will explore different levels of leadership you need to understand, and different skill sets you must master to be an effective leader.

4.1 KNOW YOUR ROLE

The "New Guy" Leader

Great! You have a title – now what? This subsection is written for either a first-time leader or the excited leader coming into a leadership position in a new organization. This will not be the only information you could need, but if you put these into practice, I can guarantee that your road will be much easier, and your journey will be much more successful. So, push your ego out of the way and prepare to learn lessons here so you don't have to weather as many sleepless nights wondering whether you were cut out for this. Let's begin!

First, when you walk into the room understand that your title only gives you a foot in the door. Once you walk through that door, the rest is on you. EVERYTHING you do from this moment on will either build trust with those that you lead, or it will build a wall of distrust that will undermine nearly everything you seek to accomplish. A wise leader will walk into a room and listen before they speak, they will assess before they seek to change, and they will seek to

Learning the Art of Effective Leadership

understand before seeking to be understood. When you first enter that new office, room, or command post, look for one crucial piece of information. Who is the existing leader? Notice I did not say "former" leader, I said existing.

Unless you are forming a team from scratch, someone currently on that team has been acting as the leader. Now that you are on site, knowing who this person is will be critical to your success. One indicator you can look for to determine who this person is, is by watching the reactions of the team as each member speaks. There will be one member of the team that stands out from the others. When they speak, everyone listens. They might all laugh at a bad joke or they might simply stop what they are doing to get a better understanding of what this person thinks on a particular subject. It's as if their own opinion depends on the opinion of this team member before they will step out and share it in public. Regardless of how long it takes to identify this person, you must identify them. Once you do, be intentional about interacting with them and understanding them. Win them over, and the others will follow.

The second thing to know is that as the "new guy," everything you do will be suspicious until you have won the trust of your team. You start with a title, but unless you take the time to understand your team and what motivates and inspires them, you are facing an uphill battle with each change to the pre-existing norm. This step requires an upfront investment of time, but when you understand your team and what drives them, you can now initiate some key productivity improvements to garner buy-in and not resistance.

Undoubtedly you will run into that person that refuses to get on board with anything new, but the overall rate at which you can accomplish great things will increase—as will the bond within the team. Skip this relational step and you will regret it. Once your team is operating on all cylinders with trust being the norm, you can more easily discern who the potential leaders are and develop them in a very intentional way. This step is where the longevity of your leadership—even your organization—is realized. The great thing about this understanding is that the cycle never changes. You will likely find yourself at a different place with each team member and each time a new member is added to the team, you start from the beginning with that person, but if you follow this basic cycle, you are off to a great start in your leadership journey.

The "Promoted Above Your Peers" Leader

This subsection is targeting those working shoulder-to-shoulder with your peers until one day you are asked to lead them. Some unique dynamics to this situation must be understood to successfully lead your peers. First, understand that not all of your peers want you to succeed. This may sound strange and is not intended to encourage you to be paranoid, but go into this situation with your eyes wide open. There will be others on your team that want to do what you have been asked to do. They may never admit it to your face, but they are shocked that you received the promotion above them and they will resist you often just to see what you've got. Others on your team will want you to succeed, but they will have a hard time seeing you as anything other than your friend. This will be most apparent when they make light of your serious moments with the team or they cut corners around the requirements you have given the team. It's as if they think that because of their previous relationship with you, you will not hold them to the same standard and that you will not have the hard conversations with them you will have with others. These team members are dangerous.

It's this mentality that will divide the team into an "us vs. them" situation where mistrust will run rampant and accusations of unfairness and favoritism will breed. Oddly enough, it's these "friends" that will act hurt and surprised when you bring them into correction, but will fail to recognize how their manipulation is hurting the team. I recommend being very direct and to confront this mentality the moment it's detected. Left unresolved, this will destroy the team. Being obviously impartial in all circumstances is the key to winning the trust of your peers in this scenario. It will not be a fast process. Leadership does not change who you are, it merely reveals who you are. Your team must see that your title did not change your character. Your methods and responsibility may change, but the central values you hold most dear will be tested like no other time before and they must stand firm. Do this, and you are off to a great start.

The "I Inherited This Mess" Leader

Sometimes as leaders, we are thrust into a scenario where we are tasked with cleaning up someone else's mess. The prior leadership employed none of the helpful things discussed in this book and the group you are asked to lead is in shambles. This is a volatile situation where your trustworthiness and your willingness to listen will be your foot in the door. Sometimes the situation was created by incompetence, while other times the situation was created by malicious intent. In either case, team members are bound to be hurt, frustrated, confused, and defensive. In these circumstances, I highly recommend gathering the team around for a quick pulse on their perspective of the organization.

- What are key areas they see that need to be addressed?

- Are there any outstanding expectations or unfulfilled promises you need to be aware of?
- What does this team feel they are doing well?
- What are they most proud of?

Until you have a full grasp of the situation and perspectives on the team, it's wise to understand that you have only a limited understanding of how the team got to where it is. I would caution against making any necessary decisions you know will rock the boat. Instead, immediately solving one or more of the team's top concerns will go a long way in the journey to building their trust in you as a leader. Without their trust, all you will get is their baggage. The more baggage you must take with you to your destination, the more it will cost in time, energy, and treasure to haul.

The "Long-Distance Relationship" Leader

This leader is becoming more common with today's technological advances. There are leaders charged with leading teams of people scattered all over the place—rarely getting face-to-face opportunities with their team members. This can be a very difficult position to be in when leadership challenges arise and hard conversations are required. My recommendation to this leader is to dedicate time discovering ways to connect visually with your team members. Relying on email or text messages as your sole platforms for communications will not be enough. There are video technologies available that can help with this, and a quick internet search will reveal many options. However, reserve the most sensitive conversations for legitimate face-to-face meetings. This will require both time and travel, but just because your team is located outside of your physical daily location doesn't mean your presence in their lives is any less powerful.

The "I Said You Could Do It, But I Want To" Leader

We have all seen this leader. Hopefully, none of us are this leader. This leader has control issues. The organization chart to this leader speaks less to empowerment and more to clarifying who they can blame. This leader loves to give tasks, criticize performance, and ultimately do it themselves. This leader believes there's only one way to properly complete something – their way.

If you are this leader, please stop. Many leaders like this don't realize it until a real self-assessment happens and they grasp how much is on their to-do list. Understand that you have a team around you. This team will fail you. You will fail your team. This is part of growing together. Failure is not something to be feared, it's something to be learned from. When a team knows that they are trusted enough to fail and grow through it, the team grows. When the team does not feel trusted, the team no longer feels empowered. If you have leaders under you, let them lead. It will be better for you and better for everyone else involved. If you know that you have a team with you that will allow everything to burn if they have that much control, get a new team.

The "Indecisive" Leader

Indecision, hesitation, and frustration are three friends that often run together. They also make poor playmates and typically chase away productivity, momentum, and profit. You cannot lead out of insecurity. Shore up your weaknesses, and if you cannot bring yourself to make "the call", then empower someone on your team to make that call. Once the call has been made, stick with it. Leaders with a high capacity will not stay in a place of limbo. Leaders with a high capacity will try to bring stability to the chaotic decision-making process, but if they are not allowed to do so, they will leave. Find a coach or mentor that will help push that fear out of you. You simply cannot keep great people around you if you cannot decide whether to trust them.

The "I Really Don't Want to Be a Leader" Leader

I get it. Sometimes we did not ask to be put in a position of leadership. Sometimes we don't feel as though we can carry out the requirements laid out before us. Do yourself a favor though, and either rise to the challenge or go play a different game. There are too many lives completely dependent on the leadership above them and their families for you to be content collecting a paycheck while being unwilling to step up and lead. What did you say? You didn't ask for this? Well, neither did your team. If you have any integrity in you, either have the hard conversation resigning your position or commit to becoming the best leader you can be by learning and growing at every opportunity. Don't allow your future, and the future of everyone on your team, to be held hostage by an unwillingness to do the right thing.

The "I've Seen It All" Leader

This will likely be the shortest subsection in the entire book. If you are the leader who has been around for a long time and have seen it all, done it all, and have nothing else to learn, I have only one recommendation for you. RETIRE. Your team can only grow as much as you will grow yourself. If you can be taught nothing, then you should be leading nothing. That is all.

The "Worn-Down" Leader

If you don't read this anywhere else, read it here. I get it. I understand. Sometimes, the weight and loneliness of leadership seems to be much more than it's worth, but trust me–don't give up. You wouldn't feel this weight if greatness were not in you. Bad leaders don't care. Bad leaders don't learn and improve… but **you are not a bad leader**. You're trying to learn by reading this book, and this likely wasn't your first stop. Leaders like you and I aren't everywhere. We're a rare breed. For us, it's not all about the money. For us, it's about more than numbers. For us, seeing the "light bulb moments" in those that we lead is why we exist. We get energy from seeing those that we lead succeed. But it's draining, isn't it? If I'm resonating here, know that you're not alone. Make sure you're building time into your schedule for you. No matter how good of a leader you are, you must refuel. When was the last time you dedicated eight consecutive hours to do something that gives you life and invigorates you? Do that soon. The organization you lead depends on it. You, whether you see it or not, depend on it more than you might realize. Refresh, Recharge, Re-engage. You can do this!

4.2 GETTING BUY-IN

Without buy-in from your team, nothing productive happens.

You can cast an amazing vision all day long. You can have the most solid implementation plan that mankind has ever seen. You can even have a successful marketing campaign attracting attention and interest in your organization that cannot be measured in mere thousands of people, rather millions of people who now know of your brand and your amazing work. You can have all of that and more, but without buy-in from your team, you are going nowhere. Often, leaders will make the mistake of trying to lead out of their insecurity. Rather than involving the team in the creative process, the leader secludes themselves—only allowing in those that will affirm what the leader wants to hear. When this happens, the level of buy-in from the team is nearly non-existent.

When the team is excluded from the creative process, the team is excluded from ownership. It then becomes a sales-pitch to garner excitement and buy-in from the team. This is like trying to scale a mountain without the proper tools. If the right tools are in place at the beginning of the journey, the process is much easier—even enjoyable! If you involve the right members of your team early on, this empowers these team members with the ability to help craft buy-in among the other members of your team as they are no longer championing "your" vision, but they are championing "our" vision. There's simply nothing like promoting something that you had a hand in creating.

Simply involving them in the creative process isn't enough, though. Each involved team member must have specific tasks they feel the weight of fulfilling. They must be held accountable for fulfilling that task to the highest of standards. Anything worth celebrating is worth fighting for, so now is not the time to be lenient on the standards.

Consider the elation felt when a member of the U.S. Army successfully completes basic training and can march in their final graduation parade. No longer just a recruit, they have earned the right to be called a soldier. That honor did not come without many hours of hard work and mental fortitude. If it had, it wouldn't mean so much today. In the same manner, the creative process can, feel like a battleground. Be glad it's so! This means that the finished product on the other end of this struggle is likely something that the team members can champion with pride for years to come.

Don't be fooled into thinking that buy-in only applies to your vision, though. Buy-in starts with you–their leader. If the team doesn't believe in you, they won't believe in whatever it is you're trying to sell them. This is why the core values discussed in the first chapters of this book are so critical. Your team isn't interested in learning your creed, but your creed should simply explain how you lead. When they hear about your core values, it should make perfect sense because the team members see these values played out every day. If you want to have legitimate buy-in from your team, you must both understand and be okay with the simple truth that what you do matters just as much as what you say.

One final note on getting buy-in from the team. If you want to maximize the team's potential, they must know that you care about them as individuals—as mothers and fathers, husbands and wives—more than you care about the work they do for you.

If you want buy-in during the hard times, you must cultivate a sense of togetherness during the good times.

This means that you're asking about their vacations, their dreams, their goals, their families and it means that you're not asking about these things, so you can manipulate them later. You're asking because you genuinely care about helping them fulfill their own aspirations. If a team member knows that you will do all you can to help them achieve *their* dreams, they will reciprocate and do all they can to help you in your quest to fulfill your vision.

4.3 MOMENTUM

Momentum, like one's reputation, is difficult to build and easy to lose. The larger your team or organization is, the faster you will notice this. Picture momentum as an old locomotive. The force required to take that massively-heavy object and move it from a complete standstill to a state where it has a continual progression of forward movement is significant. That required force is called "starting resistance." This level of force is much greater than the level of force required to keep that locomotive moving on the rails. This "rolling resistance"

Learning the Art of Effective Leadership

is much easier to maintain without expending massive amounts of resources to do so.

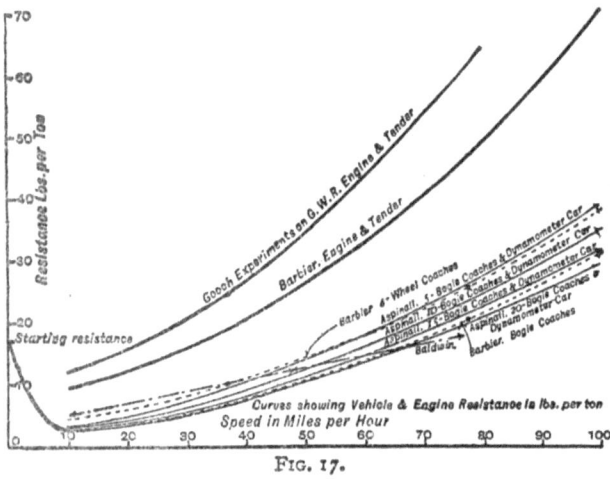

Figure 1 Train Resistance Graph A, Vol. 22, pg. 844, Encyclopedia Britannica 1911

Learning the Art of Effective Leadership

Momentum in your organization is much the same. It requires tremendous energy, effort, determination, and intentionality to launch a new product, offer a new service, market a new idea, or initiate a culture shift. Once this shift is well underway, steering the movement is relatively easy if you pay attention to keeping the systems healthy that are needed to keep your momentum on track.

Further into this section, we will explore key elements needed to maintain your momentum, but first, it would be beneficial to look at what a leader can do to build momentum. Unfortunately, there's no one-size-fits-all approach to building momentum, but a few principles will apply in every attempt to gain momentum.

Cast Vision

How you communicate the vision you are pursuing is the first critical step in creating momentum in your organization. Do you speak about your vision as though It's important, or do you talk about this vision as though it were a hobby or just another task on your to-do list?

Vision steers the organization and points it toward its destination.

Take time to refine the vision to something you can understand and communicate. If your vision does not encompass everything about you, you have the wrong vision. Vision is not simply a desire to earn more money or sell more product. Vision is what will inspire people to invite your product into their lives. Vision is what will motivate. If your vision does not inspire and motivate you to alter your behavior and to pursue things with a greater fervor, your vision is not powerful enough to generate momentum. As a leader, you must have momentum in yourself before you can build it in others.

Catch the Vision

Vision starts with the leader, but cannot be only the leader's responsibility. Naturally the leader sees first, but the leader cannot be the only one that sees, feels, and champions the vision behind the organization's efforts. So, how do you help your team to catch the vision you are speaking about? Most importantly, you must live it out. Your team must see this vision is important enough to you that it inspires change in you before you require the change of them.

Change is initiated because it's inspired, or because it's required.

Required change is fleeting. Inspired change creates a legacy. If your vision is supposed to last beyond you, create a legacy of inspired change, not a culture of required behavior modification. This inspiration does not come through memos or motivational posters, team-wide emails or contentious staff meetings, or a variety of high-pressure tactics designed to push your team to success. This inspiration comes from personal interactions that leave your team feeling that their lives are better simply because you were around them. The "come and follow me" approach has been, and will always be, a more effective leadership model than the one that says "go and do."

Define the Win

Does your team know what it looks like to score a touchdown? It's one thing to start a football game with a team of veteran players who know the ins-and-outs of the game where the fundamentals are well-rehearsed, and the rules are understood. It's something entirely different when a team full of rookies who don't know the rules of the game. With a team full of new players, they may not understand your lingo. If you tell them to score a touchdown, that makes sense to you, but do they even know what the end zone is? When leading, you don't have the luxury of assuming that your team understands what you are asking. Take the time to teach them. It's not enough to simply repeat the instructions, you must show them what it looks like to carry those instructions out. Fail to do this, and you are not fulfilling a basic requirement of good leadership–setting your team up for success by ensuring they have the resources they need to succeed.

Create the Win

Once that win has been defined, a leader wanting to build momentum will create a scenario where the team can feel what it's like to win. The team must know that their effort is paying off, so use this to your advantage– and don't take a long time in doing so. This team win is critical to create quickly after the win has been defined. This can look a lot of different ways, but intentionally creating a scenario or allowing the team to carry out what was defined for them will develop and grow their understanding of the win, their confidence in their ability to complete the win, and their enthusiasm in pursuing the win.

This is not the place to let your creativity as a leader go by the wayside. Be creative in what scenarios are presented and how the win can be achieved. The goal here is not to teach them *what* to think, but *how* to think. Let the team explore their options, create their own strategies, and own the process of the win. This will produce a higher-capacity leader and will help to fuel the momentum you are looking to first create, then sustain.

Celebrate the Win

Each win should be celebrated. Each celebration need not be a massive ordeal, but taking time to congratulate your team adds value to the team members as people and gives a much-needed mental break and a boost in confidence before tackling the next challenge. Make this an intentional time among your team. Highlight top performers. Highlight mentalities you want to see replicated. Celebrate barriers that have been broken. Celebrate your team growth. Do this, and watch your team grow like never before.

To reiterate, create momentum in your organization by doing the following in rapid succession:

Casting Vision

Catching Vision

Defining the Win

Creating the Win

Celebrating the Win

Repeat the above steps often.

Once momentum is behind you and continual forward progress is happening, steering the movement is relatively easy if you pay attention to keeping the systems healthy that are needed to keep your momentum on track. One particular system you should keep focus on is the system that fuels your organization. This fuel will be different for each organization, but keeping an ample fuel supply for your organization is critical. Just like in your car, if you fail to keep adequate fuel in your vehicle, you will stop forward momentum on the interstate system you should be traveling toward your success.

Write your answers to these questions:

1. What system provides your organization with fuel?

2. How do you know whether the fuel system in your organization is healthy?

3. When looking at this fuel system, what is going well?

4. What about this system must be improved?

5. What steps will you take to improve this system?

4.4 Starting Over

There are times as leaders we must face the harsh reality that what we are doing simply isn't working. This can result from many factors, but after you have tried what feels like every solution known to mankind, we are faced with whether to continue. Sometimes, we don't have to figure this out. Sometimes, someone figures this out for us and delivers news that we need to start over somewhere else. This section is not designed to provide the answer to whether or not you should keep pushing toward your original goal or move on to the next thing, but instead, this section will address what to do if you start over.

Admit That You're Starting Over

One of the hardest things that a leader can do is to admit that they got it wrong. This is especially true for the leader carrying out the vision they birthed and not just carrying out someone else's vision. The natural inclination for most individuals is to hold on to what is known – even if it's not working. If you are starting over, that means you must let go of those things you did that got you where you are. If they were working, you wouldn't be starting over, right?

Hold a Funeral for the Past

This may sound extreme, but the principle here is to take intentional time to celebrate the journey that got you here. Once that is done, bury the past methods, frustrations, and baggage. Put to death your "woulda coulda shoulda" thoughts. They will only get in your way later. Not that you should not learn from your past experiences, but don't live in the past. If you spend all of your creative energy fixing the past in your imagination, you will have no energy to imagine and think on what's next.

Refresh, Regroup, Re-engage

Don't jump right into the next thing. Take time to clear your mind. Do something that brings you joy in life and fuels YOU–not your organization, not your next idea–you. Set a timeline for you to renew your mind and stick with it. Find an area to grow in. Devote time to something you are passionate about, but not leading. Reignite that creativity that keeps you feeling productive. You will know when you have that creative spark again. Once you do, and the ideas flow, it's time for you to regroup.

Gather your thoughts, take a realistic assessment of the lessons learned from the last venture, and explore the new idea and what it will take to get it going. Once you have the information you need to confidently step out into this new path, take a deep breath. Exhale. Now get back into the fight.

4.5 KEY QUESTIONS

Can you identify as one of the leader types discussed in this section? If so, which one?

If not, how would you describe your current starting point in your leadership role?

Using the information in this section, what should your next steps be to chart the course to your destination?

5 U.S. Army NCO Creed

No one is more professional than I. I am a noncommissioned officer, a leader of Soldiers. As a noncommissioned officer, I realize that I am a member of a time-honored corps, which is known as "The Backbone of the Army". I am proud of the Corps of noncommissioned officers and will at all times conduct myself so as to bring credit upon the Corps, the military service and my country regardless of the situation in which I find myself. I will not use my grade or position to attain pleasure, profit, or personal safety.

Competence is my watchword. My two basic responsibilities will always be uppermost in my mind—accomplishment of my mission and the welfare of my Soldiers. I will strive to remain technically and tactically proficient. I am aware of my role as a noncommissioned officer. I will fulfill my

Learning the Art of Effective Leadership

responsibilities inherent in that role. All Soldiers are entitled to outstanding leadership; I will provide that leadership. I know my Soldiers and I will always place their needs above my own. I will communicate consistently with my Soldiers and never leave them uninformed. I will be fair and impartial when recommending both rewards and punishment.

Officers of my unit will have maximum time to accomplish their duties; they will not have to accomplish mine. I will earn their respect and confidence as well as that of my Soldiers. I will be loyal to those with whom I serve; seniors, peers, and subordinates alike. I will exercise initiative by taking appropriate action in the absence of orders. I will not compromise my integrity, nor my moral courage. I will not forget, nor will I allow my comrades to forget that we are professionals, noncommissioned officers, leaders!

About the Author

Zebulan Hundley has a Ph.D. from North Carolina College of Theology with specialization in Church Leadership. He is currently the Executive Pastor at Hope Church in Warner Robins, Georgia and has produced podcasts focused on leading volunteers within non-profit organizations. He resides in Hawkinsville, Georgia with his wife and children where they run Fire Branch Farms. He enjoys hunting, fishing, and rooting for his favorite sports teams – the Kansas Jayhawks and the Kansas City Chiefs.

Follow me on Social Media:

Facebook: www.facebook.com/zebulanhundleyauthor

Instagram: @zebulanhundleyauthor

Contact:

(478) 273-0175

info@zebulanhundley.com

www.zebulanhundley.com

www.ingramcontent.com/pod-product-compliance
Lightning Source LLC
Chambersburg PA
CBHW031919240526
45464CB00021B/579